HOLOCAUST BIOGRAPHIES

Oskar Schindler
Righteous Gentile

Jeremy Roberts

THE ROSEN PUBLISHING GROUP, INC.
NEW YORK

Published in 2000 by The Rosen Publishing Group, Inc.
29 East 21st Street, New York, New York 10010

First Edition

Library of Congress Cataloging-in-Publication Data

Roberts, Jeremy, 1956–
Oskar Schindler / by Jeremy Roberts.
   p.   cm.—(Holocaust biographies)
   Includes bibliographical references and index
   ISBN 0-8239-3310-5
   1. Schindler, Oskar 1908–1974 2. Righteous Gentiles in the Holocaust—Biography—Juvenile literature. 3. World War, 1939–1945—Jews—Rescue—Juvenile literature. 4. Holocaust, Jewish (1939–1945)—Juvenile literature. [1. Schindler, Oskar, 1908–1974. 2. Righteous Gentiles in the Holocaust 3. World War, 1939–1945—Jews—Rescue. 4. Holocaust, Jewish (1939–1945)] I. Title. II. Series.
  D804.66.S38 R63 2000
  940.53'18'092—dc21
  [B]
                            00-027846

Manufactured in the United States of America

Contents

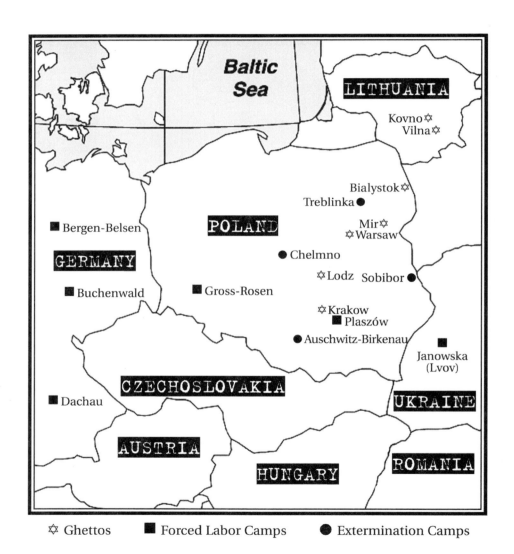

Baltic
Sea

LITHUANIA

Kovno ✡
Vilna ✡

Bialystok ✡
Treblinka ●

POLAND

Mir ✡
✡ Warsaw

■ Bergen-Belsen

● Chelmno

GERMANY

✡ Lodz   Sobibor ●

■ Buchenwald   ■ Gross-Rosen

✡ Krakow
■ Plaszów

● Auschwitz-Birkenau

■
Janowska
(Lvov)

CZECHOSLOVAKIA

UKRAINE

■ Dachau

AUSTRIA

HUNGARY

ROMANIA

✡ Ghettos   ■ Forced Labor Camps   ● Extermination Camps

Introduction: A Red Dress

The little girl runs through the crowd, her red dress sparkling with life in the dull cloud of grays on the city street. A few minutes later, we see the girl again, tossed on a heap of the dead, her dress red as blood. The young child has joined the millions murdered in the Holocaust.

This famous scene from the movie *Schindler's List* touches us with the horror of the Holocaust. The girl could have been any one of us. The man who sees the dress in the movie also could be one of us, but only if we had somehow managed to perform good deeds during dark times. For the character in the movie is based on an actual man, Oskar Schindler.

Naturally, the real Oskar Schindler was different from the movie character with his name. But like the movie character, the real man saved more than 1,000 Jews. Oskar Schindler was a hero. He risked his life at a time when few others dared to take action. But what kind of a hero was he?

No Saint

Oskar Schindler was many things: playboy, womanizer, bon vivant, scoundrel, slime. Such words all accurately describe a man who drank far too much and regularly cheated on his wife. They all describe Oskar Schindler. He was no saint.

And yet, the same man would prove to have depths of courage and humanity rare at any time—and even rarer in the times during which he lived. In ordinary times, Oskar Schindler might have been seen as a villain and worse. During the Holocaust, in places such as Poland, Germany, and Czechoslovakia, he was a saint walking through hell.

Liam Neeson (*center*) played Oskar Schindler in the movie *Schindler's List*. The real Oskar Schindler was not always an admirable person, yet he proved to have great depths of courage and humanity.

He was, as the Jews he saved would later say, "a righteous Gentile."

1. Love and Hate

It was spring, a season of hope and rebirth. The mountain region of the old empire was just coming back to life after a long winter. Everything in the town of Zwittau seemed to be alive and full of promise. And so, when the Schindler family welcomed a new boy into the family on April 18, 1908, his proud father and mother had high hopes for him. They named him Oskar.

The family was an important one in the small town. They were well-off. Oskar's father, Hans, owned a factory that produced farm machinery. There was every reason to think that the futures of both the young boy and the town were bright.

But the world around Oskar Schindler was changing rapidly. By the time he was ten, the

Oskar Schindler grew up in the region of Moravia, which became part of Czechoslovakia.

countries of Europe had fought a terrible war. Millions of people had died. Whole cities and towns had been destroyed. The Austro-Hungarian Empire, which Zwittau had belonged to for many years, was dismantled. Zwittau's ancient connection to Austria and nearby Germany was cut. The town became part of a new country called Czechoslovakia.

Czechoslovakia included many different people in its 50,000 square miles. The region

that Oskar and his family lived in was part of
Moravia. It also was part of a region called the
Sudetenland. Many ethnic Germans lived
there. They shared the customs and language
of Germany. Oskar, like many children in the
Sudetenland, went to a special German school.

Oskar had a great deal of fun growing up.
By the time he was a young man, he loved
driving nice cars and going to parties. As a

As a young man, Oskar Schindler enjoyed driving nice
cars. In this photo, he poses with his father, Hans,
in a roadster outside their home in Zwittau.

teenager, he raced motorcycles against professional drivers. He was an excellent racer. He was also known as a carefree party lover and future businessman.

The world, meanwhile, had grown dark. By the end of the 1920s, all of Europe was in a depression. Times were very difficult, especially in nearby Germany. People had a hard time finding jobs and food.

It was during this time that the Nazi Party began to gain popularity in Germany. Led by Adolf Hitler, the Nazis appealed to people for many different reasons. Many people believed that the party could end the tough times. The Nazis promised to reform the economy. Other people liked the Nazis because Hitler wanted Germany to be a strong, proud nation again. They were bitter because Germany had lost World War I. The victorious Allies had treated Germany harshly after the war. Also, many Germans liked the Nazis because the party leaders hated Jews. These people blamed Jews for all of Germany's troubles. They even said Jews should be removed from Germany.

Anti-Semitism

Jews were persecuted in Europe for centuries.
This persecution took many forms. Sometimes
they were made to live in certain areas.
Sometimes they were prevented from
holding important jobs. Sometimes they
were driven out of their homes. And
sometimes they were murdered.

Adolf Hitler salutes passing troops at the third
Nazi Party Congress.

Historians still debate exactly why anti-Semitism became so popular in Germany and the rest of Europe during the time Oskar was growing up. But there is no doubt that it was very widespread. Non-Jews took it for granted. One historian writes that anti-Semitism was "common sense."

The caricatures of Jews were not very logical or consistent. On the one hand, they were considered dirty and not quite human. On the other hand, many people thought Jews were very rich and wanted to destroy the countries in which they lived . These were crazy, but dangerous, stereotypes that had nothing to do with reality.

Hitler's Plans

Even before he became popular, Hitler laid out his plans for Germany. He did this in speeches and in a book called *Mein Kampf* (*My Struggle*). One of the most important parts of his plan was to reunite Germany with other areas that had been connected with it in the past. Some of these areas had been lost during World War I. Others, such as Austria and the Sudetenland, were connected to Germany through history and culture. In fact, Hitler thought most of northern Europe rightfully belonged to Germany, or should be controlled by Germany. He and other Nazi leaders were prepared to fight a war to achieve their goals.

Hitler and the Nazis also wanted to remove Jews from Europe. At first, they may not have known exactly what they wanted to do with them. Some Nazis wanted Jews to settle on an island near Africa called Madagascar. Eventually, Hitler and the Nazis would settle on a plan to exterminate all Jews. This was called the Final Solution. The Final Solution may not have been definite until the 1940s. But from the very beginning, Hitler and the Nazis felt Jews were subhuman and should be treated as such. Robbing, assaulting, or murdering a Jew was not a crime in the eyes of the Nazi Party.

A Nazi

There were Nazi Parties in other countries besides Germany, including Czechoslovakia. Oskar joined up during the 1930s.

It is not easy to say how much of the Nazi philosophy Oskar ever believed. It is impossible to say whether he was ever an anti-Semite. He lived in an area where there was a great deal of anti-Semitism. But there were also Jews living there, and as a boy he had Jewish friends. He does not seem to have been very active in Nazi politics. The only thing that is clear is that Oskar preferred going to parties to participating in politics.

Oskar in Love

As a young man, Oskar was expected to follow in his father's footsteps. Through the 1920s and early 1930s it seemed as if he would. The factory was going strong despite the tough economic times.

One day he and his father went to Alt Moletein in Moravia to sell electric motors. Along the way, Oskar met a young girl named Emilie Pelzl and fell in love. It was a warm day in autumn, just after the leaves had changed. Emilie fell in love immediately, her soul pierced by Oskar's blue eyes. Oskar was tall and handsome. He had broad shoulders, a trim body, and a way of making everyone he met like him. Oskar fell for Emilie as well. Their fathers seemed to have been against them marrying. Even so, they wed on March 6, 1928, near Zwittau.

Emilie said later that they were deeply in love. But the pattern of their marriage was set very early. In those days, it was common for the father of a bride to give a dowry. This money was supposed to help the young couple get started in life. According to Emilie, Oskar spent the dowry—100,000 Czech crowns, a lot of money at the time—on a luxury car and parties. Not long after the marriage, he began to cheat on Emilie. He dated other women and made love to them. Emilie did not like this, but she accepted it.

Oskar seems to have had many positive attributes. He was generous and kindhearted. But he was not very good with money, and he often acted irresponsibly. Emilie said he acted more like a big kid than a grown man.

Czechoslovakia Annexed

Meanwhile, dark storm clouds gathered over the Schindlers and the entire European continent. The Schindler family business went bankrupt in 1935. Oskar began working as a salesman. Hitler and the Nazis gradually took over Germany. As Hitler grew more powerful, he made it clear that Jews would have no place in the new Germany, which he called the Third Reich.

Oskar joined the German counter-intelligence service in the 1930s. This was called the *Abwehrdienst* or simply *Abwehr*. Belonging to it was illegal for Czech citizens. He was a spy for Germany. He was working as a salesman and frequently traveled throughout Czechoslovakia and nearby Poland. Being a spy, of course, was a dangerous job. Oskar seems to have loved the danger and adventure. He gathered most of his information simply by talking to people. He was good at making people think he was their friend. He was also good at drinking a lot and having fun. These qualities helped him to be a good spy.

According to Emilie, Oskar helped to obtain the Polish uniforms which were used by

In the 1930s, Schindler (*second from left*) became a spy for the German counter-intelligence service. He was good at gathering information from people by charming them and gaining their confidence.

German agents in Poland. She also said that Oskar's adventures almost ended when he was arrested as a spy by the Czech authorities. Luckily for him, she added, Germany invaded Czechoslovakia soon after his arrest in 1939. Not only was Oskar freed, but he was in a good position to take advantage of the rapid changes taking place in Europe.

Peace Possible?

In the summer of 1939, many people believed there was still a chance for peace. In addition to part of Czechoslovakia, Hitler had taken over Austria. He also was persecuting and murdering Jews. But many people outside these areas believed, or at least wanted to believe, that the Nazis would stop their campaign to annex territory and eliminate the Jews. On September 1, 1939, the world had to confront the reality of World War II.

2. Death Everywhere

The dawn exploded with piercing screams. Waves of Stuka dive-bombers, equipped with special sirens, attacked Poland relentlessly on September 1, 1939. They came without warning, leading the way for long columns of tanks and men. SS soldiers dressed in Polish uniforms—perhaps based on designs Oskar Schindler had helped to steal—pretended to attack a German radio station. This was used as an excuse for the invasion. Other German soldiers parachuted behind Polish lines, where they helped trick many Poles to their deaths.

Hitler's invasion of Poland was an easy rout. Krakow, a large city in the south of Poland, fell within a week. The Polish capital, Warsaw, held out for three weeks. But there was no stopping the Germans. With their powerful air force,

In September 1939, Germany invaded Poland,
shattering hopes for peace in Europe.

tanks, and infantry, they had created a new
kind of war: blitzkrieg, from the German words
blitz (lightning) and *krie*g (war). This kind of
warfare was fast and brutal. It would soon
bring much of Europe under German rule.

Jews Persecuted

Long before the war, there had been a great
deal of anti-Semitism in Poland. "It was not

21

easy for a Jew to be a student in Poland," wrote Malvina Graf many years later. Graf lived in the Krakow area before the war. She wanted to study medicine but was not allowed to because she was Jewish. Her book recalls a variety of anti-Jewish activities and restrictions in Poland before the Germans invaded.

At first, Jews didn't take seriously the aims Hitler had expressed in *Mein Kampf*, but they soon had reason to. Even before all of Poland had surrendered, the Germans created councils to oversee Jews in the areas of Poland that Germany controlled. These were called Jewish elders or *Judenrat*. In Krakow, the council consisted of twenty-four men. They had been important men before the war. The Germans used them to rule the Jewish community. The *Judenrat* oversaw the distribution of food and other necessities. It also helped establish the special Jewish police force, or *Ordnungsdienst*, which was called the OD.

The conquering Germans immediately persecuted Jews. They treated them as slaves.

The conquering Germans persecuted Jews in Poland, as they did in Germany. In the photo above, Jewish businessmen are forced to parade down a street in Leipzig, carrying signs that read "Don't buy from Jews. Shop at German stores!"

The Gestapo, which was a special German police force, ordered Jews to clean up the city of Krakow after it was captured. They forced them to fill in ditches and pick up rubble from bombed-out buildings. The work started on September 22, which happened to be the eve of Yom Kippur. It was a very holy time for Jews. Ordinarily, no work was performed then. But anyone who did not follow German orders was likely to be shot on the spot.

Things quickly got worse. Synagogues were stripped of art and religious items. Furniture and equipment was stolen from Jewish-owned businesses. Soon those businesses would be either closed or confiscated.

On October 26, 1939, the Germans announced an order called *Zwangsarbeitergruppen*. Basically, the order allowed Jews to be used as slaves. The *Judenrat* had to draw up a list of all men and women between the ages of eighteen and fifty-five. This list made it easier to organize slave labor. But it also made it easier to deport Jews or to kill them in large numbers. Before the end of the year, all Jews were made to wear armbands made of white cloth and printed with a Star of David. These identified them as Jews.

Jews were kicked out of their homes. Many were robbed of all their belongings by German soldiers and officials. Sometimes these thefts were random, done by individuals. At other times they were organized by German leaders.

The Nazis forced Jews to wear identifying armbands.
The photo above is of a woman in the Warsaw ghetto.

Any Jew could be attacked at any time for no reason. Jewish children were forbidden to go to school. Finally, part of the city was walled off. Only Jews could live there. This area was called a ghetto and it was very crowded. Often one room was shared by several families.

When the ghetto was created in December, 1939, there were approximately 80,000 Jews in Krakow. The Germans decided that, to stay in

After a deportation *aktion* in a ghetto, groups of Jewish men were assigned the task of clearing out the homes of the deported.

the ghetto, Jews would have to work. Anyone who didn't have a job—including children and older people—had to leave. Eventually, only 15,000 Jews were left. The others were transported away—often to their deaths.

Seeking His Fortune

Some German businessmen followed the army into Poland. They hoped to make a fortune. Among them was Oskar Schindler. Because of the German invasion, many businesses that had been owned by Poles were being taken over by Germans. In some cases, Germans stole factories and businesses from Jews. Sometimes they dressed these thefts up with legal paperwork. Sometimes they did not.

Oskar had been in Krakow many times before the war. He had come as a businessman and a spy. Oskar seemed not to have known what type of business he would get into when he arrived. But he probably wanted one that could make things for the German government and military. That would mean a steady supply of orders—if a factory owner knew the right people.

Oskar knew the right people. All he needed was a factory. At first, he was interested in textiles, perhaps to make uniforms or clothes. But he eventually settled on Rekord, a Polish factory that made enamelware—kitchen pots, pans, dishes, and utensils made of metal and covered with paint or enamel. Rekord had gone bankrupt, but it still had some of its equipment, such as metal presses. It would need much work and new equipment, but it had potential. Enamelware could be sold to the army, which needed plates and utensils to feed its soldiers. Enamelware also could be easily sold on the black market, which would bring even higher profits.

Oskar obtained Rekord through a German court. He leased it instead of buying it. He paid very little money for the business. He got the money for the lease and the new equipment from Jewish businessmen who had been ruined by the invasion. In return for their investment, they would receive a certain amount of kitchen items. These items could then be sold. Such arrangements were illegal, but they were not unusual. In better times, no businessman would make such a deal. But with the new oppressive laws, Jews faced losing their life savings. They also faced losing their lives. Such deals let Jews obtain goods for money that they were not allowed to use. And, of course, the deals benefited people like Oskar, who got much cash for little work.

Abraham Bankier, a Jew who had been the office manager of Rekord, helped Oskar to arrange the deals. Oskar renamed the company Deutsche Emalenwaren Fabrik— DEF for short. He soon had contracts from the German Army for field kits (sets of dishes and utensils) and some other items. Oskar was able to obtain these contracts for several reasons. For one thing, the army needed such supplies. Secondly, he had been able to obtain the factory very cheaply and would use very cheap labor—Jews. Jews did not have to be paid the same amount as Poles, let alone Germans.

What was the SS?

Although many parts of the German government and military played a role in the Holocaust, the most important unit was the SS. SS stood for *Schutzstaffel,* or guard unit of the Nazi Party. Members swore personal allegiance to Adolf Hitler. They remain a symbol of oppression to this day. "Their uniform was black and they were the terror of the nation," writes author Heinz Hohne in his book on the SS, *The Order of the Death's Head.* Heinrich Himmler headed the vast organization during the war. Among the units were the feared Gestapo, a special secret police group with enormous powers. The name came from combining two German words—*geheime staatspolizei*—which meant secret state police. Another important SS unit was the SD—*Sicherheitsdienst,* or security service. SD members worked with yet another branch of the SS, known as *Einsatzkommandos,* to liquidate Jews in Poland and elsewhere. These missions eventually led to the creation of extermination camps.

SS units ran the work and extermination camps and were responsible for carrying out the Final Solution. At its peak, as many as one million men were part of the SS.

Therefore, Oskar could sell the items for a cheaper price than others could.

But the most important reasons that Oskar got the orders was because of his friends—and bribes. Oskar knew many people in the German army and SS. He constantly went out of his way to meet people with influence who could help him. He used his charm and his contacts to get contracts.

He would also bribe people in obvious and not-so-obvious ways. For example, someone who did Oskar a favor might receive free sets of enamelware that could be sold on the black market. That person also might be invited to lunch or dinner to have a good time. Oskar was a good salesman, especially when he was selling himself. He had a way of making people like him. Part of it was on purpose, of course—he wanted people to like him so that they could help him to get rich. But part of it was just in his nature.

DEF did well, especially at first. Oskar expanded the factory from about forty-five people to more than 250 by the summer of 1940. Most, though not all, of his employees were Jews.

Oppression Worsens

Persecution of the Jews worsened during this time. The population continued to shrink for many reasons, including murder. German soldiers and officials who killed Jews were not considered murderers.

To many outsiders, Oskar certainly would have appeared to be one of the persecutors. He used slave labor in his factory. He was getting rich thanks to crimes such as bribery and selling things on the black market. He partied a lot, and lived in an apartment that had once belonged to Jews. He had at least one mistress and drank huge amounts of liquor. But he would soon do things which made it obvious that there was another side to him. These actions would place him in grave danger. They would also save many lives.

3. A Kiss of Death

The German businessman and playboy seemed to be mocking him. Itzhak Stern was a proud man, and though he found it necessary to work with the Germans for survival, he had his limits. Stern was an important member of Krakow's Jewish community. He was an accountant and business manager, intelligent and judicious. But these were dark, difficult days for all Jews. So when Oskar Schindler paraded like a fool in front of him that December day in 1939, Stern did not object, but merely listened. Schindler had come to visit Stern's boss, and stopped on his way out.

"Tomorrow it's going to start," said Schindler, according to the account in Thomas Keneally's book, *Schindler's List.* He seemed to be boasting. "Jozefa and Izaaka Streets are going to know about it."

Stern thought it was just another idle German boast. Anti-Semites were always calling Jews dogs and worse, saying that they would soon be put in their place. The threats were meant to intimidate them, nothing else. But when the area that Schindler had mentioned was cleared of Jews the next day, Stern began to realize that Schindler had meant the words as a warning. He had told

Ben Kingsley (*right*) as Itzhak Stern assembling the list of Jewish workers to be placed under Schindler's protection, in *Schindler's List*.

Stern of a planned *aktion* designed to rob, harass, and eliminate Jews in that area of town. It was one of the first large-scale, organized persecutions of Krakow Jews.

The Ghetto

The Nazi plan for the Jews of Krakow—and all of Europe—evolved as the war went on. But from the very beginning, Jews were seen as subhumans. They were to be confined to special areas. Ultimately, they would be eliminated, either through deportation or death. In this way, Germany and then Europe would be "cleansed."

In Krakow, a section of the city that had traditionally had many Jewish residents became the ghetto. It was officially established in March 1941. The Nazis had been persecuting Jews for many months by then. Jews had been confined to different areas of cities throughout European history. But the Nazi ghettos were different. The Krakow ghetto was sealed off with new walls

A barbed wire fence separated the ghetto in Podgorze
from the rest of Krakow.

and barbed wire. There was nothing voluntary about living there. Any Jew who was found outside the ghetto without very special permission was liable to be shot. The ghetto was not expanded to let more people live there. On the contrary, less and less space would be allotted for the ghetto area as time went on. Many families and individuals had to squeeze into apartments meant for one family.

Above all, the ghetto was meant as a temporary holding pen, not an area where people might enjoy life. The only way to stay in the ghetto was to have a job. Anyone who did not work for either an approved industry or the German government would be forced out. They would be sent to a concentration or death camp. That included children as well as adults.

Other cities throughout Poland had similar ghettos. Life inside the ghettos was very difficult. Food was very expensive and often hard to find. Valuables often had to be sold just to survive—if the Germans didn't steal them first. At any moment, an *aktion*, a raid by German troops, could mean death. Any Jew could be humiliated, beaten, or even killed at any time. But life outside the ghetto was impossible. Jews were only allowed to live in the ghetto, no matter where they had lived before the war.

"SS men passing in ghetto streets attacked and kicked Jews at random," wrote Malvina Graf in her book, *The Krakow Ghetto and the Plaszów Camp*. "They would frequently grab elderly religious Jewish men and shave their sidelocks and beards."

The sidelocks and beards were important symbols for these men. Shaving them off seemed like the ultimate humiliation. But many worse things could, and did occur.

What Schindler Did

In this atmosphere of uncertainty and death, people sought shelter and help wherever they could. Oskar Schindler's warning, as well as his willingness to hire and help Jews

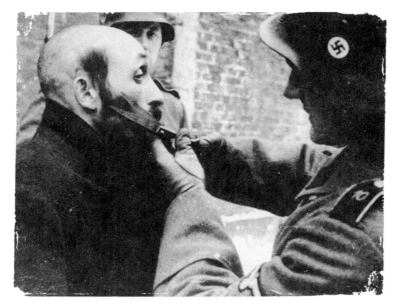

Jews living in the ghetto were subject to public humiliation by SS men.

in small ways, convinced Stern and others that he might act as a friend to Jews. Stern began working with Schindler in December 1939. He gave Schindler advice and helped him to make connections with different people in the community. He eventually came to work at DEF. Stern and Oskar also became friends.

With the help of Stern and many others, DEF expanded and became very profitable.

Besides kitchenware, Oskar added a section to the factory to produce shell casings for German weapons. This section of DEF may never have been very successful. There is some question about whether the ammunition it created was any good. But it helped Oskar in many ways. For one thing, it made his factory more important to the German government and army. And the more important the factory was, the more important Oskar was.

Oskar had not come to Krakow to save Jews. He came to become rich. Stern and others did not help Schindler to make him rich. They helped him to help themselves. As Stern's nephew Menahem Stern told a journalist years later, Stern used Schindler as much as Schindler used his slaves. Because the only way to stay in the ghetto—and to stay alive—was to have a job, Jews needed DEF to survive. They needed Schindler, because he could provide them with jobs. That saved their lives—and earned him large amounts of money.

Beyond Mutual Benefit

From the time of his very first warning to Stern, however, Oskar took more risks than were necessary. He seemed to want to help Jews, at least a little. Oskar lied to the German authorities many times. Against regulations, he hired people at the factory who were not skilled. He tried to make conditions in his factory good for the workers. He paid for extra food out of his own pocket. He bought it from the black market and provided it illegally. He prevented German authorities from harassing his workers. He protested when SS men pressed his people to shovel snow instead of coming to work. Doing these things put him in great danger.

Not that he didn't have fun. He had a lot of it. He brought his wife to Krakow and also kept two mistresses there. He spent large amounts of time going to parties and drinking, often with Nazi murderers. He drove expensive cars and lived like a very rich man.

Slaves

When the Krakow ghetto was officially created in March 1941, the status of Jews changed once more for the worse. No wages could be paid to Oskar's workers. Instead, their fees had to go directly to the SS. All the Jews would receive was food and housing rations. Jews were now complete slaves.

Oskar appeared uneasy about this change for many reasons. Although it saved him some money, he was uncomfortable with slavery. Author Thomas Keneally suggests that Oskar knew the war eventually would end and that he thought about the aftermath of the American Civil War, during which slaveholders were punished. On the other hand, Stern and others asked

Other Employers

Oskar Schindler's factory was not the only one to use Jews as slaves. Large German companies such as Krupp and I.G. Farben used and abused Jews. In the Third Reich, Jewish labor was used to make everything from metal cables to steel and aircraft.

Schindler (*second from left*) with his office employees at DEF (Deutsche Emalenwaren Fabrik).

Oskar to take on more workers. Slaves or not, only Jews with jobs could be saved. Oskar agreed.

Oskar lived near the ghetto and passed by it often. The walls were covered with signs denouncing the Jews as bandits and worse. Among them was a poster of a Polish girl giving food to a caricature of a Jew in the shadow of the devil. "Whoever helps a Jew helps Satan," read the slogan. It was a sign Oskar must have seen nearly every day.

A Success

In the spring after the ghetto was established, Oskar took a trip back home to Zwittau. His wife had returned there. His aunts and his sister lived there too, and his mother's grave was there. He wanted to see them all.

The one person he didn't want to see was his father, Hans. Oskar and his dad had not gotten along for many years. Oskar thought his father was very harsh toward him. Hans Schindler had divorced Oskar's mother before her death in the 1930s. Oskar never forgave him. They hadn't spoken for many years.

One night while in a café talking with friends, Oskar saw his father in the next room. Friends pushed the two men together. Keneally imagines the scene in his book, *Schindler's List.* He believes that Oskar must have been surprised to see his father make a friendly gesture toward his son. It was almost as if the old man was admitting he had been wrong. It was a moment of reconciliation for Oskar and his father. It was also a moment of triumph. Oskar Schindler had become a rich man.

All for a Kiss

On April 28, 1942, Oskar celebrated his thirty-fourth birthday in grand style. He managed to buy bread on the black market for the DEF workers as a treat. He gave out small gifts like cigarettes and passed out cake. He shook hands and even kissed the girls.

The next morning a black Gestapo police car roared down the street and skidded to a stop in front of the factory. Two agents met Oskar in the factory yard and told him he was under arrest. Oskar pretended that he wasn't worried. But as he was led to jail he realized that he was in serious trouble. He had been questioned the year before because of his black market deals. A few phone calls to the right people—and some bribes—had quickly gotten him out of trouble. But now things were serious. He was taken to a jail where prisoners were routinely tortured and killed. The charge: kissing a Jew. It was a race crime. It could be punished by death.

For five days, Oskar sweated out the detention. Outside, friends worked desperately to secure his release. Finally, an important policeman arrived to question him. Fortunately, Oskar had met the policeman before. Oskar admitted that he had kissed one of the Jewish girls, but he told the policeman that it was because he had been drinking.

The policeman wasn't that interested in the crime. All he wanted was a sizable bribe— kitchenware that could be sold on the black market. Oskar gladly arranged it.

4. Horrors and Sanctuary

On October 28, 1942, all the Jews of Krakow were ordered to assemble in a small plaza in the middle of the ghetto. They soon found themselves subjected to the harshest *aktion* the ghetto had ever seen. The Germans told the Jews that no identity cards were necessary—the first sign that this roundup was very serious. No one was allowed to go to work. A few people hid, but they risked instant death if they were caught. The entrances to the ghetto were sealed off, and the highest Nazi leaders were present to supervise the proceedings.

The people were formed into two groups. One group contained mostly people who worked outside the ghetto and seemed to be in good health. The other included mostly people who were old, or unable to work, or young, or just unlucky. One of Malvina Graf's sisters was selected for the second group. She tried to protest that she had a job but was beaten on the head. The Jews in the second group were marched out of the ghetto. A few in this group, including Malvina's sister, were saved by a Nazi officer. He saw some Jews who worked for him and ordered them to his office. The rest either were killed outright or were transported to camps.

The October *aktion* was designed to drastically reduce the Jewish population. It was part of a plan to eliminate the ghetto. Over the next few months, all of the Jews left alive in Krakow would be sent to a new work camp on its outskirts. There, they would work as slaves until they died or until they were no longer able to work—at which point they would be killed. The camp, located at the edge of Krakow, was called Plaszów. Part of it was built over a Jewish cemetery.

Plaszów

The different *aktions* in the ghetto had left people like Malvina Graf numb. By now,

A U.S. soldier stands next to a pile of coffins in the gas chamber at Dachau. The fake showerheads that dispensed the gas can be seen above.

they had heard that some of the camps that the Germans had established were not prisons or work camps. They were for large-scale murder. At places like Treblinka or Auschwitz-Birkenau, hundreds of Jews at a time could be herded into gas chambers. They were poisoned and their bodies shoveled into furnaces and burned. Work camps were better, but only by comparison.

49

People there were still likely to be killed at any time. The Germans meant to work them until they were no longer good for work. Then they, too, would be killed.

In December 1942, the Krakow ghetto was divided in two. One section was for people who had jobs. Everyone else was assigned to the second section. It seemed obvious that everyone in the second section would be deported and killed. Gunshots were sometimes heard by people in the other ghetto. There were random roundups of people in both places.

The OD

Inside the ghetto, a Jewish police force was set up to carry out German laws. The Jewish police force was called the OD, short for *Ordnungsdienst*. OD members took their orders from the Gestapo. Sometimes the OD bent the rules. Sometimes they enforced the rules ruthlessly. While OD members sometimes enjoyed special privileges, most were eventually killed by the Germans.

Members of the OD wore armbands and badges in the shape of the Star of David. They assisted in deportations, but when the Krakow ghetto was liquidated, OD members were themselves deported to the Plaszów labor camp.

As work on the Plaszów slave camp continued through the winter, life in the ghetto became harder and harder. The streets were deserted during the day. No one wanted to be caught by a sweep. Everyone worked, trying to hold onto the scarce jobs open to them.

51

Oskar the Spy

Sometime in the late fall or early winter of 1942, a dentist came to Krakow and happened to look up Oskar. Soon after the man walked into Oskar's DEF office, Oskar realized the meeting was not accidental. The dentist had something on his mind besides teeth or dishes. He had been sent by a secret Jewish organization that operated in Budapest, Hungary, and other areas outside of Nazi control. He wanted information on what was happening to the Jews in Poland. Oskar told him no one would believe it. He hardly did himself. And then, after a drink, Oskar calmly laid out what he knew of the Final Solution.

It was clear to Schindler by this time that the Nazis had decided to completely eliminate the Jews. This was not to be done merely by random murder or by placing Jews in ghettos or concentration camps. Death would be organized and performed in the manner of an assembly line. The dentist found the story barely credible. But he had to believe what he heard. Oskar Schindler was a German who benefited greatly from Nazi policies. He had no reason to lie about this.

The dentist somehow managed to convince Oskar to travel to Hungary to tell others in the secret group what was happening. Oskar risked his life to get to the secret meeting by hiding in the back of a truck. He told the people he met about the extermination camps, where large numbers of Jews were being killed. He also gave other details about what was going on. The men urged Oskar to go to Istanbul, Turkey, where he could tell others about the Final Solution. Despite the dangers, he eventually agreed. He also agreed to help pass money to be used for bribes to free Jews in Poland. This was an even greater risk than traveling to meet the underground group.

At the end of this meeting, Oskar and his secret contact went out drinking at a nightclub. For Oskar, the dangers of spying and the Holocaust were always mixed in with parties and booze. He acted rashly in nearly every way possible.

A Sadist

The fat man's naked belly hung over his belt. A cigarette hung from his lips. He wore a small, funny-looking hat from his native mountains in Germany. Under other circumstances, he might have seemed like a clown, prancing on the porch of his house, except that he had a rifle in his hand. He took

Amon Goeth was the sadistic camp commandant of Plaszów. He frequently used his rifle to shoot prisoners for sport.

Children First

When they were selecting Jews for death camps, Germans nearly always chose old people and young children first. Many, many children under twelve were killed. They could not be worked to death in the labor camps and served no useful purpose in the Nazi war effort.

Some children did manage to survive in the camps, however. Their mothers, fathers, and other adults hid them. Some German guards and officials also must have helped, at least by pretending not to notice. There are accounts of guards warning that children should be hidden during inspections.

aim at a woman a few yards away from him and fired. The woman fell to the ground, dead. The other workers stared back at him in horror, but he only waved at them to get back to work. Apparently, the man had decided to kill the woman just because he could.

The man was the commandant of Plaszów, Amon Leopold Goeth. He arrived in Krakow in February 1943. His job was to set up and oversee the camp. He was an SS *Sturmbannführer*, roughly the equivalent of a major in the U.S. Army. Goeth ruled absolutely and despotically.

Men and young boys in concentration camps worked as
slave laborers and lived under brutal conditions.

Anyone who displeased him for any reason was likely to be shot. That included a street cleaner who didn't bow to Goeth when he passed. It also included any Jew who happened to be near him when he was in a bad mood. Young, old, male, or female, it made no difference. Goeth had an entire crew of killers at Plaszów, though few were quite as sadistic as he was.

At its peak, about 25,000 people were imprisoned at Plaszów. While the Germans wanted industries to locate in or next to the camp, many, like Schindler, stayed behind in Krakow. Each day workers would be assembled and then marched or transported to their work sites. Six watchtowers, electric fences, barbed wire, and concrete poles and barriers formed the boundaries. Jews lived in wooden barracks. They slept in boxlike bunks. Toilets were in separate buildings far away. The inmates of Plaszów were constantly beaten and whipped as punishment for any offense.

But lashings could seem like a kindness compared to other forms of punishment. One day Goeth began questioning a man about his identifying papers. When the man didn't answer the way Goeth wanted him to, the commandant told the man to run. The man realized he had no choice but to obey. As soon as he did, Goeth released the two dogs he kept as pets. They tore the man to pieces and began eating him. The dying man's screams were silenced by a bullet to the brain. Goeth walked away, letting the animals finish their meal.

Oskar's Camp

As a prominent German businessman in Krakow, Oskar met Amon Goeth soon after he arrived. The two men quickly formed an understanding and an odd kind of relationship. Oskar often attended parties at Goeth's camp quarters. He also gave the commandant heavy bribes. But he seems to have despised Goeth for many reasons, not the least of which was his murderous sadism.

Oskar quickly realized that he did not want to relocate his factory inside the slave camp. He knew that, contrary to promises, Goeth would quickly interfere. Soon after most of the ghetto was liquidated in March 1943, Oskar launched a new plan. He decided that not only would his business stay in Krakow, but he would try to bring the workers there as well. If Jews were to be kept in a work camp, why not his? He schemed to create a satellite camp behind the DEF plant. He bought land behind the factory for the camp with his own money. He somehow managed to persuade Goeth to go along with the idea—if he could obtain permission from the SS generals above the commandant.

Oskar rounded up supporters in the German government. He argued that he lost much work time because the workers were kept so far away. He bribed numerous people to get his camp okayed. German laws did permit such subcamps. Still, it is not precisely clear how Oskar was able to obtain permission to build his. Certainly he used all of his powers of persuasion, from bribes to chatting up people at parties. Author Thomas Keneally points out several other reasons why SS officials might have gone along with the idea. Oskar would pay for the new camp. The new camp would give the SS room for more Jews in other camps. There would be ample opportunities to skim rations and supplies meant for Oskar's camp. Many people, including Goeth, would profit by selling these illegally.

Compared to Plaszów, the DEF camp was a paradise. Sometimes called "Emalia", after

Ralph Fiennes (*left*) played SS commandant Amon Goeth in *Schindler's List*. Schindler persuaded Goeth to go along with his idea for a satellite work camp at his factory.

the factory name, it had a shower and a laundry. There was much more to eat there than at Plaszów. In fact, a doctor said later that daily rations came to about 2,000 calories, roughly a normal diet. Above all, there were no random killings or floggings. Workers put in twelve-hour shifts at the factory. But the work was far easier there than at Plaszów.

The camp housed workers for other factories, not just Oskar's. There were roughly 900 inmates. Besides spending his own money on extra food for them, Oskar regularly bought liquor and other items to bribe SS guards and inspectors who might cause trouble. He intervened several times, both at the factory and at Plaszów, to save prisoners from torture or death. He also helped to buy the freedom of other Jews in Poland, working with the underground group. And as always, he went to parties with his friends, his mistresses, his business associates, powerful German officials—and criminals like Amon Goeth.

5. Dust in the Wind

During the spring and summer of 1944, death began to loom over the Third Reich. On the eastern front, the Russians drove the Germans back and began marching toward Germany itself. By early June, the Allies would land in Normandy. Death fell over Krakow, as well. It fell in the ashes and soot that covered the city from Plaszów to DEF to the posh palaces of the local Nazi chiefs. It came from the bodies dug up from Plaszów's killing fields. It covered everyone, as if blanketing the living with guilt.

Oskar didn't need to feel the ashes or see the funeral pyres to know that the end was near. He had a steady supply of informants in the German military who told him how badly the war was going. As a German businessman, Oskar would certainly be in danger if the Russians captured him. He also had to fear the Germans, and not only if he was caught helping Jews. Anyone with information about what had really happened in the camps could be killed.

The Jews, of course, were in even more danger. Not even Oskar's workers were safe. The SS might order a last frenzy of death before Plaszów was dismantled. As other camps were dismantled, their prisoners were marched or shipped by train further west or simply were killed. And so Oskar reached a decision, which he told Stern: he would rescue them all.

Gambling for a Life

Somewhere toward the end of the summer, orders arrived for Plaszów—and Oskar's subcamp at DEF—to be disbanded. The men were to be relocated to a rock quarry camp called Gross-Rosen, where they would be worked to death. The women would go straight to Auschwitz-Birkenau, where most would likely be killed soon after they arrived.

Oskar was by then hard at work on a relocation plan of his own. He hoped to move the factory to his native country of Czechoslovakia. He claimed to be interested in continuing to manufacture armaments. But his real goal was simply to escape with all his workers. He began making a list of workers and others he would take with him.

The entrance gate at Auschwitz was inscribed with the motto "Arbeit Macht Frei" (work makes one free).

One night he went to Amon Goeth's house to play cards. Goeth kept losing. Finally, when Goeth was heavily in debt, Oskar suggested they play for new stakes—Goeth's maid Helen Hirsch. The maid had endured many months of toil and torture, working for the commandant. It was obvious to Oskar that Goeth would eventually kill her. He had tried to free the girl before but had failed. "She'll go to Auschwitz anyway," Oskar said. He put up double Amon's debt against her life on one hand of blackjack, or twenty-one—a simple card game. In twenty-one, the player who scores closest to twenty-one points without going over wins. Face cards, such as the king or queen, count as ten points. An ace can count as one or eleven. Goeth finally agreed. He dealt the cards.

Oskar got an 8 and a 5. Thirteen. He asked for another card. A 5. Eighteen. A good score— but enough for a life? Another, said Oskar. He got an ace. Nineteen. It would have to do.

Goeth turned over his cards. He had a three and a five and dealt himself a four—twelve.

Less than Oskar. He had to take another. He turned it over, hoping for a nine or an eight. He got a king. Twenty-two points—over the limit. Oskar had won Helen for his list.

Schindler's List

In the fall of 1944, Oskar traveled around looking for others to join him in his escape plan. He also hunted for a place to escape to. He found an old textile plant near his hometown at the edge of Brinnlitz. He spread money liberally to get the necessary approvals. Keneally reported that Oskar estimated he spent about $40,000 "to grease" the transfer, or make it possible.

In theory, Oskar was going to make anti-aircraft artillery shells at the new factory. He claimed that every worker on his list was a highly skilled craftsman or munitions worker. In reality, he had no intention of making weapons or ammunition. And few if any of the Jews were munitions experts. In the meantime, the war continued to go badly for the Germans. Amon Goeth was arrested by superiors in the SS, probably because they suspected him of illegal dealings.

Working with the help of Stern and others, Oskar completed his list. About seventy names of workers from another man's factory were added at the last minute, along with the names of some others Oskar knew. He presented it to the authorities for approval. At some point, some names may have been added to the list by a personnel clerk, Marcel Goldberg. Some of the camp survivors who talked to Keneally and others years later accused Goldberg of adding names to the list in exchange for bribes. In some cases, names may have been crossed off the list. At least one of the men who managed to survive blamed Oskar for taking him off the list, though it is difficult to say exactly why his name was crossed off.

Roughly 1,100 people were on the list when it was approved by the German authorities. The authorities thought that they were sending the Jews to a new camp. Oskar and the Jews believed they were escaping hell.

Salvation

On October 15, 1944, the men on Schindler's list were taken to a railroad siding at Plaszów. There were about 800 of them. Their train included about 1,300 men bound for the rock quarry camp—and likely death. For three days, they traveled south. The weather was cold. Each car had a single bucket of water. Finally, they came to a halt.

SS guards appeared. "Everyone out!" they shouted. "Strip!" The prisoners shivered as they took off their clothes. And then they realized they weren't in Oskar's camp. They were in Gross-Rosen, the quarry camp. Naked, they stood outside for the night and much of the next morning. Finally they were led to showers, given uniforms, and fed a pittance of bread. Then they were put back out on the marching grounds to stand at attention for another ten hours. Finally, on the third day, they were put back on trains and sent southeastward, to Czechoslovakia.

Brinnlitz

Oskar busied himself overseeing preparations for the camp and the new factory. He also renewed his relationship with his wife. There are conflicting stories about how their love fared during this period. Some note that Emilie Schindler was at the Brinnlitz factory only during work hours. They say the pair seemed cool towards each other. But in her memoirs, Emilie gives the impression that their marriage revived. Whatever they felt toward each other, both worked hard to help the workers and other Jews with whom they came into contact. As her husband did, Emilie risked her life to save many people.

It must have seemed obvious by then that the war would end in defeat for Germany. But the Nazi government and military were still in control of things. Oskar paid for the construction of the camp, the relocation of the factory equipment, and new supplies for the Brinnlitz complex. He also paid many bribes to SS officials. And he paid the SS "wages" for the workers—who at this point had no work to do. Thomas Keneally estimated that the wages came to roughly $14,000 a week for the men, with another $4,000 for the women. But the women hadn't arrived when they were supposed to. In fact, Oskar soon feared that they might already be dead.

Auschwitz-Birkenau

The women had boarded a train with inmates from Plaszów inmates that stopped at Auschwitz-Birkenau. This massive complex in western Poland consisted of two main centers. One was Birkenau, where Jews stopped first and were separated into two groups. One group was sent on to Auschwitz, which contained concentration and work camps. These "lucky" Jews were greeted by forced labor, harsh treatment, torture, and murder.

The others were gassed and killed immediately at Birkenau. There was one way to tell if you were "lucky" or not: the SS

Jewish slave laborers in concentration camps had
identification numbers tattooed on their arms.

tattooed Jews who were to be sent to
Auschwitz to work. The Nazis wanted to
keep track of the living. There was no need
to keep track of the dead.

When they arrived at Birkenau, the women
on Schindler's list were not tattooed. They
were taken to a windowless brick building. All
around them, other Jews were being led to the
gas chambers, or shot. Many of "Schindler's
Jews" gave up hope.

71

As soon as he realized what had happened, Oskar began working to have the women released. But he hadn't gotten very far when he was arrested by the Gestapo.

A Prisoner's Threat

After his arrest, Commandant Goeth had apparently told the SS that Oskar bribed him to "go easy on" Jews. Oskar was questioned about this by SS investigators and a judge. He denied that he had bribed Goeth, but he did admit that he might have loaned Goeth money. He told them that Jews with special skills were useful to his business. To ensure that he got the man or woman he wanted quickly, he "loaned" the commandant money.

Oskar kept mentioning the fact that his work was necessary for the German war effort. He hinted that Goeth had extorted money from him, though he may not have said so directly. But corruption wasn't his biggest problem. In the eyes of the SS, his association with Jews was more serious than any bribe. The SS officials suspected he was more than a slaveholder. They thought he liked Jews. To like a Jew, let alone to save Jews from death, was a crime.

Oskar had had a great deal of practice in lying and cheating. He put his skills to good use now. But he didn't have to lie when asked whether Goeth was his friend. The answer was an unshakable "no." The questioning went on for about a week. While Oskar kept up his performance, his wife and friends were calling acquaintances for help. Finally, Oskar succeeded in getting a message to an important *Oberführer*, a senior colonel in the SS. The message made it clear that Oskar would tell the investigators he had bribed the *Oberführer* if he wasn't freed. The message may have done the trick. He was soon released.

Together Again

If his imprisonment scared Oskar, it didn't stop him from bribing SS officials. He apparently bribed some to help win the release of the women kept at Birkenau, though it is not clear exactly what happened. Some people say that Oskar sent a girlfriend to sleep with an important SS official, perhaps the camp commandant. Others say he had a woman pack a suitcase full of luxuries like booze for a much lower-level bribe. Emilie Schindler said Oskar convinced a woman who was an old family friend with influence in the SS to speak on his behalf. Other versions of the story say that Oskar himself went to speak to SS officials. These versions seem less plausible, but they may be true. They also show what people thought of Oskar after he saved them. They may capture some of the truth about his character, even if the specific facts are wrong.

In one story, Oskar was asked how a nine-year-old girl on his list could be a skilled worker. Oskar supposedly replied that the child had small fingers that could reach inside the shells to polish them. In perhaps the most incredible story, Oskar went to the camp barracks to personally oversee the women's departure. He walked among them in the assembly yard, leading them from slavery to the promised land. The German industrialist, the great sinner, seems in this story to be Moses, the great prophet, leader, and father of his people. Whatever really happened, the women were finally delivered to Brinnlitz. They had spent three months under the smokestacks of death.

6. Chaos

The factory at Brinnlitz was many things.
However, it was not a successful factory. Oskar
seems to have had no intention of really
making ammunition there. He had few, if any,
workers truly skilled in munitions. He may not
have had all the proper equipment. But he
covered this up in various ways. He bought
shells from other factories and passed them off
as his own. He claimed there were difficulties
in moving the factory. He also continued to
bribe officials, directly and indirectly. He
continued his affairs with young women. One
day workers caught him naked in a large tub
with a female SS guard. He just smiled.

The war continued. Things became more
and more chaotic. It was harder and harder to
get food. Brinnlitz was a haven. But it was not

an easy place. The Jews there were still slaves and had to work—even if the items they were producing didn't work. The living conditions were hardly pleasant. And there was always the danger that Oskar's tricks and bribes would fail. Then they would all be killed.

The End

As the winter went on, Oskar, Emilie, and others worked to save other Jews. In some cases they were able to save one person at a time. In one case, they managed to save thirty—out of a group of 10,000 they had been aiming to help. In January 1945, Oskar sent some workers to a nearby railyard. They freed 100 freezing Jews from a cattle car. They were brought to the factory and nursed back to health.

The Russians and Americans were closing in on Germany. But the Nazis continued killing Jews furiously. Even if Germany lost the war, they hoped to achieve their greatest aim: eliminating Jews from Europe. Finally, around the time of Oskar's thirty-seventh birthday, orders were issued. The Jews at Brinnlitz were to be separated into two groups. The old and the lame were to be shot right away. The others would be marched to another large concentration camp.

Oskar worked to keep the orders from being carried out. He seems to have helped to

Jews were transported to the death camps in cattle cars. In January 1945, Schindler's workers rescued a cattle car full of Jews from a railyard near Brinnlitz.

arrange the transfer of an important SS official to thwart the killings. But only the end of the war finally prevented the executions and death marches.

New Dangers

All during that spring, the Russian army advanced toward Brinnlitz. Oskar and his wife heard rumors that Russian troops were killing German civilians. Oskar faced even more danger because he was a German businessman. He had worked for the *Abwehr* and was wanted by Czech guerrilla forces. Emilie said that his name was on a list of Germans to be detained and possibly executed.

Oskar and Emilie decided that their best chance for survival lay with the Americans. The American army was advancing from the west. The Schindlers decided to head in that direction for Switzerland, which was neutral. Oskar somehow managed to obtain a luxurious two-passenger sports car intended for the Shah of Iran. On the day Germany surrendered, they

"The list is life"

The list that Oskar Schindler and his workers prepared to save "his" Jews still exists. The Israeli organization Yad Vashem has it in its archives in Jerusalem. Most of the 1,100 names or so are typewritten. Some seem to have been added after the others. Others have been crossed out.

held a tearful farewell with the Jews at the Brinnlitz factory. The workers presented Oskar with a piece of paper stating how he had saved their lives. Then Oskar and Emilie headed for the American lines. They were followed by a truck with several workers.

The Schindlers passed through a countryside devastated by war. Ruins smoldered all around them. Crowds of refugees choked the roadways. The Schindlers were armed only with their wits, Oskar's silver tongue, and a large diamond he had managed to hide in the car.

Stopped by Czech soldiers loyal to the Allies, the Schindlers escaped capture—probably because the Czechs thought they were Jews, not Germans. With the help of their former workers, they found safety in a Red Cross camp. There they spoke as little German as possible, trying not to give themselves away.

As the Russian army advanced, the Schindlers fled
to Switzerland through the devastated Czech
countryside.

All the time, a Russian unit was looking for
Schindler, the *Abwehr* spy. Finally, Red Cross
workers helped them board a train to
Switzerland. The train stopped at an American
camp, where once again Oskar and his wife
were mistaken for Jews. They kept up the
deception, realizing that their lives might
depend on it. Finally, they made it to another
train and escaped to Switzerland.

A Failure

The years after World War II were difficult for everyone in Europe. Many people, Jews especially, had lost everything—their families, their possessions, their health, and in many cases, even their hopes.

Now poor, Oskar and his wife felt that they could not return to their home village in Czechoslovakia. The Czechs there would hate them because they had worked with the Germans during the war. And when they traveled to Germany after a short time in Switzerland, they found that they were not welcome there either. They were considered foreigners.

Eventually, the Schindlers moved to Argentina, where they worked as caretakers on a farm. According to Emilie, Oskar hatched many schemes to get rich. None worked. He also continued to sleep with other women. Eventually, Oskar went to Frankfurt, Germany. He left Emilie behind. Although they never divorced, they never lived together again. By the start of the 1960s, with Oskar in Europe and Emilie in Argentina, their marriage was effectively over.

Help Comes

After the war, several Jewish organizations and the people whom Oskar had helped to escape tried to help him. They gave him money and other things. Oskar also received money from the German government for the factory that he had lost during the war. But Oskar was never able to duplicate the success he had had during the war. Most people say that he was a very poor businessman. He was certainly more likely to spend money on a party than on proper business items. Oskar had always preferred having a good time to working. He seems to have remained that way to the very end.

7. Fame, If Not Fortune

The people Oskar had helped did not keep silent about his efforts. On the contrary, they told many others about what he had done. They called themselves Schindler survivors and *Schindlerjuden,* or Schindler Jews. Oskar himself was not shy, and would talk about the war with journalists when asked, so his story soon became known.

In 1949, a Canadian writer named Herbert Steinhouse heard about Schindler's story and decided to investigate. Steinhouse met Oskar and talked to him for a long time. He interviewed many Jews who had been saved. He also witnessed a reunion between Oskar and Stern. His work may have been the first on the subject. Ironically, Steinhouse could not sell his

The sculpture pictured above is on the grounds at Yad Vashem, the Martyrs' and Heroes' Remembrance Authority in Israel.

story to anyone. It wasn't printed until many years later. Today, it is important because it helps to confirm many of the stories told later.

Yad Vashem

An agency in Israel dedicated to preserving true accounts of the Holocaust began investigating Oskar Schindler in the late

1950s. Called *Yad Vashem*, The Martyrs' and Heroes' Remembrance Authority, the organization collected evidence of his work. In the early 1960s, the Israelis declared him "a righteous person." This was a great honor. Many Jews believe that God provides the world with a few "righteous persons" who are non-Jews, known as Gentiles, to help Jews and others survive tragic times. Yad Vashem's museum and archive center includes a section dedicated to these special people.

Over the years, several stories were published about Oskar. In the 1960s, German newspapers called him "Father Courage" for his efforts. Ironically, these stories got him into trouble in Germany, where he was called a "Jew kisser." Oskar was mocked everywhere. Once he slugged a man who had been making fun of him. He was taken to court and fined. Eventually, though, the German government joined those honoring Oskar. It awarded him a Cross of Merit in 1966 and gave him a pension in 1968.

In the early 1960s, Oskar Schindler was declared a
"righteous person" by the Israeli agency Yad Vashem.
A tree was planted in his honor on the Avenue of the
Righteous among the Nations.

Oskar died in 1974, after collapsing at his apartment in Frankfurt. He was buried in Jerusalem following a triumphant, but mournful, procession through the city.

Keneally's Book

Six years after Oskar died, Thomas Keneally went shopping for briefcases in Beverly Hills, California. The store he visited happened to be owned by Leopold Pfefferberg, a Schindler survivor. It was there that he first heard of Oskar Schindler and his exploits. Keneally happened to be a writer and professor. He was from Australia and was well-known for his books. He was interested in the remarkable story, and he began to talk to others about it. Eventually, he interviewed fifty survivors. He also did research in Poland, Czechoslovakia, and Israel. The result was an impressive book published in America in 1982 as *Schindler's List*.

Keneally called his book a novel because he told the story with the tools a novelist might use, such as dialogue and detailed description. Read aloud, it sounds like a work of fiction, but it is based on fact. Keneally's book was a best-seller. It told many people about Oskar's story. And it also brought Oskar to the attention of a famous movie director, Steven Spielberg.

The Movie

Steven Spielberg's movies include *Jaws, E.T., Close Encounters of the Third Kind,* and *Jurassic Park.* He became interested in the Schindler story after reading a review of Keneally's book. But it took him more than a decade to make the movie, which he also called *Schindler's List.* Until that time, most of the stories in Spielberg's films were adventures or fantasies. In an interview about the film, Spielberg said that he needed to mature before he could begin. Only after he had his own family and spent a lot of time thinking about the Holocaust could he start.

"I've never told a story like this before," he said. "Such a serious story . . . I feel like I'm reporting more than creating. These events, this character of Oskar Schindler, and the good deeds he did at a terrible time weren't created by me, they were created by history." Spielberg's film went on to win seven Academy Awards. It was named the best film of 1993. It told the world about Oskar Schindler.

While they praised the movie, Emilie Schindler and many others pointed out that it is not 100 percent accurate. For example, they

The highly acclaimed film version of *Schindler's List* was a departure for director Steven Spielberg.

said that many of the characters are based on more than one person. Itzhak Stern's nephew Menahem told a journalist in 1994 that the character of his uncle is actually based on several people. Emilie was irked by several scenes based on the book, but which, she said, were inaccurate. Even so, she liked the movie well enough to highly recommend it.

"Although based on a book that does not always reflect the whole truth," said Emilie in her memoirs, "I thought it was an excellent film, and believe it well deserves all the awards it has received."

8. Righteous Man or Horrible Sinner?

Many accounts of Oskar Schindler's life struggle to discover the moment when he changed from a bad person to a good person. Most end by saying that no one will ever know for certain why such a sinner did so much good. It is true that no one can ever look inside someone else's head. But sometimes we can be blinded by a person's bad actions. It can be hard for us to realize that good and bad actions can come from the same source.

In Thomas Keneally's book and Steven Spielberg's movie, Oskar Schindler appears to progress from a happy-go-lucky adventurer to a flawed hero. But no one has been able to find one actual event in real life that changed Oskar. The few times he is known to have

The people Oskar Schindler helped did not forget his efforts. He is pictured above (*left*), at a reunion of *Schindlerjuden* in Munich in 1946.

spoken about why he saved Jews, he was very vague. He would only say he felt he had to.

Oskar Schindler was a very complicated man. Among the first things he did when he met Itzhak Stern was warn him about an *aktion* against the Jews. From the very start of his time in Krakow he put his life at risk for Jews. His reasons for giving the warning and for most of what he did were certainly complex. Part of

93

them must have been that he hoped to benefit. Warning Stern would show Stern that Oskar could be a friend. It might convince Stern to help him. That help would be very valuable when it came to running the factory.

But part of the reasons for everything Oskar did undoubtedly came from a genuine concern for people. Oskar Schindler loved interacting with people. He liked having friends. He liked talking and debating with them. He liked being liked. This is especially obvious in his many sexual affairs. More important, he was concerned for people on a personal level, before as well as during the war. He acted on that concern, following emotions instead of business logic. He was very free with whatever he had.

He also had always been a risk taker, starting with his early days racing motorcycles. At least part of Oskar's reason for becoming a spy for the Germans seems to have been the adventure and risk it brought. And, of course, Oskar also liked having—and spending—money.

The same personality traits that made him cut deals with German officials must have played some role in his decision to help Jews— especially the Jews, like Stern, whom he knew. People close to him, like Stern and others, must have helped influence and nurture this concern. Their words and encouragement probably made him bolder. But the seeds for his heroism were planted long before Oskar came to Poland.

A Complicated Reality

From one point of view, Oskar Schindler was a horrible man. He cheated on his wife. He associated with killers and sadists. He made a fortune by using slaves. He broke numerous laws. He corrupted many men. He stole. He profited from others' misfortunes.

From another point of view, Oskar Schindler was a savior. Through his efforts, more than 1,000 men and women, who probably would have been butchered, lived. He risked his life for others countless times. He

Compensation

The German government in 1999 decided that it would compensate Nazi slave laborers. This included people who were forced to work in German factories as well as people like Schindler's Jews who were put into slave labor camps. A fund of approximately $5.2 billion was to be set aside for victims and their survivors. Half the money would come from the government. The rest would come from large businesses that used the slaves. The plan is very complex. Details were still being worked out in early 2000.

used some of his ill-gotten gains to feed and free many people. Was Oskar Schindler a terrible sinner? Or was he a hero? He was both.

In another time and place, Oskar Schindler surely would be considered bad, perhaps evil. His good qualities would not be visible, at least to most people. In fact, he might not even have had a chance to put them to use. These qualities—such as concern for others, mercy, compassion, and courage—might have gone unnoticed and unused.

But the horrors of the Holocaust made these qualities obvious. The Holocaust may even have helped nurture them. Perhaps in another time and place, without so much evil around him, Oskar would not have tried to be so brave. He might not have tried to help and save people, because there might not have been a need to do so. He might not have stood up to the vast powers of the SS or the Gestapo or the entire German government if the ashes of the dead were not falling on his head.

Some people have questioned Oskar's motives. They say he saved Jews in order to save himself. That is difficult to prove. He risked his own life many times when he did not have to. However, there is no question that he was not a perfect person or a saint. The skills he used to save Jews—lying, cheating, bribing—were more often used for his own pleasure. If we consider him a hero, we also must consider him a conniver and sinner.

But perhaps that is the greatest lesson of his story: No matter how great our flaws or sins, we all possess the seeds of a hero. We, too, can do some good—if we are brave enough to try.

Timeline

1908	Oskar Schindler born in Zwittau.
1914-18	World War I. The effects of the war in Germany helped lead to the rise of Adolf Hitler.
1928	Oskar marries Emilie Pelzl. While they are very much in love at first, he soon begins to cheat on her.
1933	Adolf Hitler becomes chancellor of Germany. His powers quickly grow until he becomes a dictator. Nazis begin campaign against Jews.
1935	Nuremberg Race Laws passed, legalizing Nazi policies against Jews.
1938	Germans enter Austria, taking over the country. In October, they occupy the Sudetenland in Czechoslovakia. This includes Oskar Schindler's home town. Around this time, Oskar becomes a spy for Germany.

1939

Germans invade Poland on September 1. Poland falls before the end of the month. Oppression of Jews begins with the invasion. Oskar arrives in Krakow and begins looking for a business to take over.

1940

Auschwitz concentration camp is created at the town of Oswiecim in Poland, not far from Krakow.

1941

The ghetto is established at Krakow. Oskar earns a reputation as a decent employer of Jewish slaves.

1942

During January, there are mass killings at Birkenau-Auschwitz. The Final Solution has become accepted Nazi policy. Oscar, aware of the killings, gives information to Jewish underground organizations.

1943

Plaszów, a slave labor camp, is set up near Krakow. The Germans liquidate the Krakow ghetto, moving all Jews to work or extermination camps. Oskar manages to open a "subcamp" at his factory, where conditions are much better.

1944

Plaszów is closed. Oskar helps prepare his famous list. He moves his factory and the Jews to Brinnlitz in what is today the Czech Republic.

1945   With Russian troops only a few blocks away, Hitler commits suicide in Berlin. Oskar manages to save all of his workers, as well as some additional Jews. He and his wife barely escape death.

1949   Oskar and Emilie go to Argentina.

1963   After much investigation, Oskar is honored as a righteous man for his rescues and other efforts to help Jews.

1974   Oskar dies in Germany. Emilie continues to live in Argentina.

Glossary

anti-Semitism
Hatred of Jews. One of the prime causes of the
rise of the Nazis and the Holocaust.
Unfortunately, anti-Semitism has a long
history throughout the world and remains a
problem to this day.

Birkenau-Auschwitz
Massive concentration and death camp complex
in western Poland. Sometimes simply called
Auschwitz. An untold number of Jews and
others died there.

concentration camp
General term for special prison compounds
used by the Nazis and overseen by the SS.
Besides Jews, political prisoners, prisoners
of war, gypsies, and homosexuals were
among those imprisoned or killed in
such camps.

death camp

General term for concentration camps devoted to
   immediate mass murder of Jews and others.
   Also known as extermination camps.

death marches

Mass marches from concentration camps
   instituted at the end of the war. While the stated
   aim was to move prisoners from one
   concentration camp to another, many died or
   were killed during the marches.

DEF

Oskar Schindler's Polish enamelware plant. Short
   for *Deutsche Emalenwaren Fabrik,* or German
   Enamelware Factory.

Einsatzkommandos

Special units that organized mass killings of Jews
   and others. They worked as part of
   Einsatzgruppens.

enamelware

Metal items coated with special paint or enamel.
   Metal makes the item strong. The enamel
   coating prevents rust and corrosion. Such items
   can be used for a variety of purposes, such as
   pots and dishes. Oskar Schindler's factory
   produced enamelware.

Final Solution

The term adopted by the Nazi government for the plan to kill all Jews in Europe. Sometimes historians use the term to note the change from earlier stages of Nazi thinking, which may have allowed for "merely" removing Jews from Europe and not necessarily killing all of them.

Führer

Adolf Hitler. Literally, the Leader.

Gentile

A non-Jew.

Gestapo

Feared secret police unit of the SS with broad powers. The name comes from *Geheime Staatspolizei*, or state secret police.

Ghetto

A general term for any area of a city set aside for a certain group of people. Jews lived in ghettos throughout much of European history. Laws restricting ghettos and activities there have varied greatly over time. During World War II, the Germans established ghettos intended to help prepare for the elimination of Jews.

Holocaust

Term adopted by historians to describe the mass
extermination and murder of Jews by Nazis.
Estimates on the exact number killed vary, but a
common number used is six million Jews. Many
non-Jews also lost their lives as part of the Nazi
campaign to rid Europe of "subhumans."

Judenrat

Councils of Jews appointed by the Germans to
govern local Jews in their ghettos.

Nazis

General term for Germans and others who
followed Hitler. Specifically, Nazis were
members of the National Socialist German
Workers' Party, NASDAP, which Hitler led. The
party had been founded immediately after
World War I.

OD

The Jewish police force in the ghettos. Short for
Ordnungsdienst.

SS

The *Schutzstaffel* or guard unit of the Nazi party.
Members swore personal allegiance to Adolf
Hitler. This massive organization swelled to
more than one million members during the

war. The SS included the Gestapo, the *Einsatzkommandos*, and units that oversaw and guarded the concentration camps.

Star of David

A six-pointed star often used as a religious symbol. Nazi laws required Jews to wear a Star of David at all times in the occupied territories.

synagogue

Jewish house of worship. Among religious items kept in a synagogue is a scroll of the Torah, which contains the five books of Moses. These books are included at the beginning of the Christian bible, along with other Jewish writings known to Christians as the Old Testament.

work camp

Concentration camp where Jews were used as slaves in some industry or factory, which often was located within the camp. To an inmate, being sent to a work camp might mean life instead of death. But the camps were not intended to keep Jews alive forever. Inmates were be worked to death. They were disposable, like cheap machine parts.

For Further Reading

Easy Books to Read

Beyers, Ann. *The Holocaust Overview.* Springfield, N.J.: Enslow Publishers, 1998.

Frank, Anne. *Diary of a Young Girl.* New York: Pocket Books, 1953.

Meltzer, Milton. *Never to Forget: The Jews of the Holocaust.* New York: Harper and Row, 1976.

Meltzer, Milton. *Rescue: The Story of How Gentiles Saved Jews in the Holocaust.* New York: Harper & Row, 1988.

Roberts, Jack L. *The Importance of Oskar Schindler.* San Diego: Lucent Books, 1996.

More Difficult Reading

Bauer, Yehuda. *A History of the Holocaust.* New York: Franklin Watts, 1982.

Graf, Malvina. *The Krakow Ghetto and the Plaszów Camp.* Tallahassee: The Florida State University Press, 1989.

Keneally, Thomas. *Schindler's List.* New York: Simon & Schuster, 1982.

Schindler, Emilie (with Erika Rosenberg, translated by Dolores M. Koch), *Where Light and Shadow Meet.* New York: W. W. Norton, New York, 1997.

Silver, Eric. *The Book of the Just.* New York: Grove Press, 1992.

Movies and Videos

The Holocaust — In Memory of Millions, 1993. Narrated by Walter Cronkite. Documentary overview of Holocaust.

Night and Fog, 1955. Classic documentary by director Alain Resnais, still rated among the best films on the Holocaust. Subtitled.

Schindler's List, 1993. Popular film directed by Steven Spielberg.

Survivors of the Holocaust, 1995. Documentary starring Steven Spielberg and others. Includes information on why he created Shoah, a foundation to educate others about the Holocaust.

Web Sites

Yad Vashem

An Israeli organization dedicated to the
Holocaust.
http://www.yadvashem.org.il/education/index.html

American Society for
Yad Vashem

http://www.yadvashem.org

The Museum of Tolerance
http://www.wiesenthal.com/mot

Historical Timeline on
Holocaust Events

http://www.historyplace.com/worldwar2/
holocaust/timeline.html

U.S. Holocaust Memorial Museum
http://www.ushmm.org

Holocaust Victims

http://www.nizkor.org

Documents and Articles Relating to Holocaust

http://www.holocaust-history.org

Index

Index

About the Author

Jeremy Roberts has written several biographies for young
people, including works on Joan of Arc and Joseph
Goebbels.

Photo Credits

Cover courtesy of Simon Wiesenthal Center Library and
Archives, Los Angeles, CA; pp. 7, 34, 60, and 90 © Everett
Collection, Inc.; pp. 9 and 21 © CORBIS; pp. 10, 18, 43, 54,
and 87 © Leopold Page Photographic Collection, courtesy
of United States Holocaust Memorial Museum; p. 12
© Joanne Schartow, courtesy of United States Holocaust
Memorial Museum; p. 23 © William Blye, courtesy of
United States Holocaust Memorial Museum; p. 25
© Raphael Scharf, courtesy of United States Holocaust
Memorial Museum; p. 26 © Archiwum Panstwowe w
Krakowie, courtesy of United States Holocaust Memorial
Museum; pp. 36 and 64 © Instytut Pamieci Narodowej/
Institute of National Memory, courtesy of United States
Holocaust Memorial Museum; pp. 39 and 78 National
Museum of American Jewish History, courtesy of United
States Holocaust Memorial Museum; p. 49 © Francis
Robert Artz, courtesy of United States Holocaust Memorial
Museum; p. 51 © Raphael Aronson, courtesy of United
States Holocaust Memorial Museum; p. 56 © Michael
Woskowitz, courtesy of United States Holocaust Memorial
Museum; p. 71 © Israel Government Press Office, courtesy
of United States Holocaust Memorial Museum; p. 81
© Central State Archive of Film, Photo and Phonographic
Documents, courtesy of United States Holocaust Memorial
Museum; p. 85 © Nik Wheeler/CORBIS; p. 93 © Avi Granot,
courtesy of United States Holocaust Memorial Museum.

Series Design

Cynthia Williamson

DISCARD